How to Teach the Bible with Excellence: Answering the Call to the Teaching Ministry

How to Teach the Bible with Excellence: Answering the Call to the Teaching Ministry

Training from Jesus' Ministry and Methods for Mastery and Teachers of Adult Bible Learners

by Lenita Reeves, BS, MA, MBA, Doctoral Candidate

Purpose House Publishing

Copyright

Contents

Training believers with a teaching grace to serve their gift in excellence.

Chapter 1

The Purpose of This Book

---

*Go ye therefore, and teach all nations, baptizing them
in the name of the Father, and of the Son, and of the
Holy Ghost:* [20] *Teaching them to observe all things
whatsoever I have commanded you: and, lo, I am with
you always, even unto the end of the world. Amen.*
(Matthew 28:19-20 KJV)

Teaching is central to the Great Commission. Examine
various translations of Matthew 28:19-20, and it is
apparent that teaching is indispensable to advancing the
kingdom of God. The verse says, "teach all nations." It says,
"teach them to observe all things whatsoever I have commanded
you." To make disciples, someone must teach them, which means
we cannot fulfill the Great Commission and make disciples
without trained, *effective* Bible teachers.

That means if you are a Bible teacher, you are an ambassador.
Moreover, the expansion of the kingdom and the degree to which
solid disciples are developed depends on the effectiveness of your
teaching. Please stop and consider that.

I know many Bible teachers who don't feel like ambassadors.
There was a time I didn't either. In my ignorance, I felt like I was

being handed a chore. Until one day, I sat and listened to someone else teach a session of an adult Sunday School class I had been assigned to co-teach. I sat there listening, and by the end of the class, I was more confused than before. At that moment, the Holy Spirit helped me to see and understand how valuable what he had given me was—how valuable the teaching ministry truly is in the life of the Believer. If God endowed you with grace to communicate truth such that the hearer leaves with understanding—and not confusion—you are valuable to the kingdom. You are a disciple-making ambassador.

Because of a lack of proper training, many Bible teachers feel less like ambassadors and more like someone thrown into a room of sharks and forced to swim. But if you are a Bible teacher, you have joined the ranks of our precious Savior, Jesus, who had to teach in the presence of wicked men and women, the unlearned, and the unbelieving. Still, he stood strong in his message, teaching with authority as the divine ambassador sent from heaven that he was. Thank God we have Jesus as our Master Teacher and example!

Again, I say to you, you are indispensable. Other than the lead pastor of a local assembly, the persons who actively support the Kingdom's disciple-making efforts are teachers of adult, young adult, youth, and children's Bible studies, classes, or cell groups. Whether you ever stand in the main pulpit or not, your role is crucial. The kingdom needs you to advance.

I don't think you would be reading this book unless you have been involved in or affected by Bible teaching in some way and want to see your teaching ministry excel. So please know that this book was written with that assumption. It is written to you as if you have been called to the teaching ministry, and you must realize how vital your ministry is to the expansion of the kingdom.

What if the next great Kathryn Kuhlman, Billy Graham, neighborhood evangelist, or Sunday School teacher is sitting in one of your classes? What impact will you make on their lives? Every time you teach, you have an opportunity to impact the kingdom—please do not overlook your potential or take it for granted. Sit up; rise up, shake yourself, and welcome yourself once again to the teaching ministry.

Can't you remember the first Bible teacher who strongly impacted your life? You'll likely never forget what they taught you, even if you were a child the first time you heard it. That is the potential magnitude of effective Bible teaching. It has eternal implications, and *your* teaching ministry has eternal implications too. Please say to yourself, "my teaching ministry has eternal implications!" Shout it aloud!

Through years of experience, I have come to realize that every time I teach, I have an opportunity to affect eternity. That is why I love the teaching ministry and have over twenty years of Christian teaching experience as an adult Sunday School teacher, cell group leader, women's ministry leader, associate pastor, intercessory and prophetic trainer, and lead pastor. I also have over ten years of professional, corporate instructional design experience and have served as an adjunct faculty member and teacher trainer. This is important not only because it gives me the qualification to write about this topic but also because it reflects that teaching is a huge part of my life.

It is both a grace and a passion for me, so I love to see it done well. I have a passion to equip others to do it effectively and excellently; and sometimes, I'm annoyed when it's not done well. Can you relate? Most people endowed with a teaching grace can absolutely relate. They are annoyed by error or when a teacher isn't systematic in their approach. Teachers can be each other's biggest critics—not in a malicious way—we just can't help but fact-check and organize other people's sermons while they are teaching. Ha-ha! If you find yourself doing that, can spend hours researching a single Bible word or topic, or don't mind sleeping in a bed piled with books on one side, you're probably a Bible teacher, and it's good to laugh at yourself from time to time.

Moreover, if you love to see the "lights" turn on for students, that's another clear sign you're a Bible teacher. I love that, and I love seeing church members excited about the Word of God because of effective teaching. I get "joy in the Holy Ghost" when I can see illumination happening inside of them, their excitement about the Word of God they are receiving, or hear them say, "Whew, I never saw that Scripture like that before. Have I been reading the same Bible as you?" When this happens, disciples start to come alive. That's what we want; that's the result of effective, Spirit-empowered, otherwise known as anointed, Bible teaching.

Even if you don't consider yourself a Bible teacher, my passion is to make you an effective one. Yes! Every Believer must be able to teach in some capacity, whether as a parent, co-worker, or leader. Okay, okay. Granted—God may not have called them to carry the title or function of "teacher," but we should all know something about the teaching ministry. That is my passion.

To that end, this book focuses on developing and delivering Spirit-empowered Christian education for the purpose of the hearer's transformation and illumination. It is an instrument to train believers with a teaching grace to serve their gift in excellence. You will learn how to effectively teach adults and hone and develop the teaching grace that Jesus has placed inside you.

We begin with a focus on you as a teacher and branch out to help you add skill to the raw grace with which you have been endowed.

As you progress through this book, you will be able to:

- Explore the responsibilities of a Bible teacher. You'll answer questions like: Can anyone be a Bible teacher? What is required?

- Evaluate your goals and motives for the teaching ministry. You'll answer questions like: Why am I even doing this? What's the point? What should my focus be? Who is really the central focus of my teaching?

- Explore the concept of Christian Education and why its uniqueness matters.

- Discuss principles of adult learning. We'll answer questions like: Why does it matter that my audience is adults? How do I address the fact that adults have varying learning styles, educational levels, and cultural backgrounds?

- Examine Jesus as Master Teacher. We'll look at his approach and methods.

- Analyze why there is no one greater than Jesus after which to model your teaching ministry.

- Craft your personal Christian Education teaching philosophy. You will articulate your philosophy and approach for why and how you teach the Bible to others.

- Apply practical information to design a lesson plan for a Bible study or class that you and other teachers can use.

I hope you're excited and ready for what will be a wonderful journey we'll take together. Take a moment to review this chapter's key points. Then, reflect on or discuss the questions with other Bible teachers.

Chapter Key Points

- Teaching is central to the Great Commission.

- You're likely to never forget the first Bible teacher who impacted your life and what they taught you, even if you were a child the first time you heard it. That is the potential of effective Bible teaching. It has eternal implications.

- This book focuses on how to effectively deliver Christian education for the purpose of the students' transformation and illumination. You will learn how to effectively teach adults and hone and develop the teaching grace that Jesus has placed inside you.

Reflect or Discuss

1. Who was the first Bible teacher who strongly impacted your life? What do you remember about them and what they taught?

2. Do you get irritated when you must endure Bible teaching that is less than excellent or inaccurate, and why? What do you usually do when that happens?

3. How long have you been a Bible teacher? Whether you're new or experienced, what do you hope to achieve by being a Bible

teacher? What kinds of things do you hope your students gain or say about you when you teach?

In the next chapter, we begin by focusing on you as a teacher, including your personal responsibilities, habits, and expectations. Then, we'll look at the responsibilities of a teacher from men's and Scripture's perspectives. Let's get started.

Chapter 2

The Responsibilities of the Bible Teacher

---

*For as the body without the spirit is dead, so faith
without works is dead also. 1 My brethren, let not
many of you become teachers, knowing that we shall
receive a stricter judgment. 2 For we all stumble in
many things. If anyone does not stumble in
word, he is a perfect man, able also to bridle the whole
body. (James 2:26-3:2 NKJV)*

Would you find it unreasonable for a person who's never
been married to conduct twelve weeks of marriage
counseling for a married couple of twenty years? Would
you think it foolish for someone consistently in dire financial
straits to advise a multimillionaire on money management issues?
Most men and women would label this as foolishness. They
expect that if someone teaches something, they have life evidence
to endorse their credibility to teach it. In the above passage of
Scripture, James is telling us that it is unreasonable for Bible
teachers to teach what they have not worked out in action. Many
churches so desperately need help that they will let anyone teach
the children, women, or adult Sunday school. But can anyone be a
Bible teacher? James tells us that every Bible teacher is responsible
for being a doer of what they teach.

Responsibility One: Be a doer of what you teach.

Think about that. What are the implications of someone who doesn't give regularly teaching about giving or tithing? What are the consequences of someone who still uses profanity teaching others what the Bible says about bridling the tongue? James says the result will be stricter judgement. If you've ever wondered what the phrase *stricter judgement* means, you can find the answer in the following passage from Luke's gospel:

> And that servant who knew his master's will, and did not prepare *himself* or do according to his will, *shall be beaten with many stripes.* [48] But he who did not know, yet committed things deserving of stripes, shall be beaten with few. For everyone to whom much is given, from him much will be required; and to whom much has been committed, of him they will ask the more. (Luke 12:47-48 NKJV, italics added)

That may seem harsh. However, when God calls us to teach, he commits to us his Words. He gives us his thoughts, mind, and heart through revelation as well as the responsibility to dispense it to others through communication. What could be more precious? That means if you have been given a teaching grace and ministry, you have been called to represent God to his future and current disciples. You have been "given much."

Correspondingly, much will be required of you. That means a higher standard—you will be like the child that can't get away with anything and always gets caught. God will ask more of you than others, so just accept that it will not feel fair. But seeing the transformation in your students certainly makes it feel fairer.

To be a Bible teacher is to come up higher, repent quicker, and change faster than others. It is to live by example. If you embrace the Christian teaching ministry—no matter what age group you teach—you must commit to coming up higher, repenting quicker, and changing faster than others. You must cultivate genuine repentance that produces change as a lifestyle.

Responsibility Two: Come up higher, repent quicker, and change faster than others. Cultivate repentance as a lifestyle.

Now, I don't say that as one who is exempted. I say that as one who has come to grips with the weight of that truth. That is why I now understand what repentance as a lifestyle is and why we must not frustrate the grace of God by tolerating sin in our lives.

To live up to the "much" we have been given, we must let the Word of God transform us first. That means the Bible teacher cannot and must not tolerate self-deception. Again, it is Apostle James who points out, "But be doers of the word, and not hearers only, deceiving yourselves" (James 1:21 NKJV). Don't you get the sense that James had a teaching grace? He told us that if we don't commit to first letting the Word transform us before we teach it to others, we'll end up shipwrecked, and in the worst kind of deception there is—self-deception. It's the worst because you've set yourself up for stricter judgement but can't see that the very words you're teaching others are witnesses against you. It's like looking in a mirror but seeing a face masked by the make-up of self-importance instead of your true face. Yet still, you think the masked face you see is the real you.

Responsibility Three: Let the Word of God transform you first. Focus on continual transformation to avoid self-deception.

E.G. White said, "Let it never be forgotten that the teacher must be what he desires his pupils to become. Hence, his principles and habits should be considered as of greater importance than even his literary qualifications. He should be a man who fears God and feels the responsibility of His work."[1] That means transformation must be the consistent lifestyle of the Bible teacher. If you stop being transformed by the Word, the flow of fresh water that's supposed to come from your teaching gets jammed up and tainted by the flesh. Dr. Howard Hendricks calls this the Law of the Teacher, which is "If you stop growing today, you stop teaching tomorrow."[2] Secular teachers call this being a continuous learner or life-long learner. But for the Bible teacher, the emphasis must be continual transformation. As Paul said, ". . . be transformed by the renewing of your mind" (Romans 12:2 NKJV).

After he tells us we need to put action to what we teach, James warns us about our words. He says a mark of true Christian maturity is when we do not stumble in words, and to teach when we have not matured in the use of words is dangerous. Why? Teaching involves the use of words. Teaching is communicating through words primarily and by example. However, the reality is that not everyone we teach will be privy to our private lives, so our words are the first thing they "see."

Jesus said, "The words that I speak to you are Spirit and life" (John 6:63 NKJV). So then, if we have not matured in words, of what "spirit" is our teaching? That does not only mean purity and lack of profanity. Teachers have a responsibility to be mature in their language, use of words, and vocabulary while teaching. Your audience and the state of your heart should dictate those choices,

---

[1] E.G. White, *Fundamentals of Christian Education*, (Nashville: Southern Publishing Association, 1923), 58
[2] Dr. Howard Hendricks, *Teaching to Change Lives: Seven Proven Ways to Make Your Teaching Come Alive*, (Sisters, OR: Multnomah Publishers, Inc., 1987), 17

not your personal preferences. According to Matthew 12:34 NKJV, ". . . out of the abundance of the heart the mouth speaks." In a sense, teachers must know that they are always teaching by the words of their mouth, whether in the classroom setting or not, because we teach who we are—we teach out of the heart and spirit of who we are because words are spirit.

If you teach internationally, make effort to expand your vocabulary. Learn a few words in the native language of your audience's culture. It will help you break the ice and demonstrate that you care.

Responsibility Four: Be mature in your words. Discipline your tongue, mature in your word choices, and develop your vocabulary.

You are probably wondering why I didn't list "study to show yourself approved" as the teacher's number one responsibility. Well, if we don't get these heart and spirit attitude responsibilities right first, our study will be colored by self-deception and pride.

The Word of God is Spirit, and we cannot approach it with the wrong spirit and think we will get the right Spirit out of it. For this reason, I believe the heart and spirit attitude responsibilities we have discussed thus far are of utmost importance for the Bible teacher. Now, let's look at Paul's advice to Timothy.

> Do your best to *present yourself to God* as one approved, a worker who does not need to be ashamed and *who correctly handles the word of truth*. (2 Timothy 2:15 NIV, italics added)

This Scripture is loaded with insight. It reveals that the first person the Bible teacher should present themselves and their teaching to is God. "Do your best to present yourself to God . . . who correctly handles the word of truth" (2 Timothy 2:15). When we present ourselves to God, we must remember that he is never impressed by our teaching. Every revelation, insight, understanding, or ounce of wisdom we get from Scripture comes from his Spirit, and his ways and thoughts are infinitely higher than our ways and thoughts.

We must never become impressed by ourselves or our teaching. Instead, we must seek to be able to stand before him and please him. We must be diligent—we must put in the effort to stay on the right side of the line and walk in humility and harmony with the Spirit of the Scriptures.

Responsibility Five: Before you present your teaching to men, present yourself to God. Focus on pleasing him, not impressing men.

Paul goes on to tell Timothy that he should correctly handle the Word of Truth. This implies that there is an incorrect way to handle it, and we must labor to stay on the correct side of the line. There is sound doctrine, correct motive, laborious study, Holy Spirit illumination, accurate cultural context, and harmony in congruent Scriptures on the correct side of the line. Dogma, tradition, misuse of Scripture for personal and denominational agendas, error, and isolated interpretations are on the wrong side of the line.

A Note Concerning Proper Study Tools

Proper tools are needed to stay on the right side of the line of Bible study and interpretation, and correctly handle the Word of Truth. The basics tools of Bible study include:

- A Study Bible in a translated version of the Bible—not a paraphrased version of the Bible, and preferably one translated by a committee to ensure checks and balances. Paraphrased versions of the Bible, like *The Message Bible,* are not direct translations, which means words or language may be added for emphasis that was not in the original text.

- An additional version of the Bible to clarify meaning and context. The Bible is not an American, Latin, or African American text. It was breathed in the spirits of Hebrews surrounded by Gentile cultures; the cultural influences of the phrases and times are key for understanding. I suggest the *NIV Cultural Background Study Bible* by Zondervan because it is loaded with cultural research and history that helps the Bible teacher understand the cultural context of the Scriptures. Also, the NIV translation was done by a committee.
  - o If you opt for another secondary Bible, add *Manners and Customs of the Bible* by James M. Freeman to your arsenal for cultural context.

- A Strong's Exhaustive Concordance with Hebrew and Greek Lexicon. This allows you to research the original meaning of words in Scripture in their Hebrew or Greek native language.

- A Bible Dictionary, like *Vine's Complete Expository Dictionary of Old and New Testament.*

- An English Dictionary such as Merriam-Webster or Oxford Dictionary.

- A set of Bible maps. When the Scripture says things like "He must needs go through Samaria," do you know where Samaria is in relation to Jerusalem? Consult a Bible map.

Some people recommend Bible Commentaries, but I am not a fan. I prefer to ask the Holy Spirit to give me commentary and review commentaries only after I have studied and heard from Holy Spirit. If you do opt to use Bible Commentaries, I recommend using them only after your personal study and questioning/inquiry with the Holy Spirit. Also, note that many commentaries are colored by the biases of their authors. Use caution.

A Note Concerning a Bible Study Method

Another aspect of employing proper tools is having an approach or method of Bible study. How do you approach your study of the Bible? What do you do when you sit down to study? I recommend the Inductive Bible study method as a solid approach to studying the Scriptures that relies on the Holy Spirit.

One of my favorite graphic handouts describing the Inductive Bible Study method is from Precept Ministries and Moody Bible Institute. You can find the handout at the link in the footnotes.[3] It explains that the three steps of Inductive Bible study are observation, interpretation, and application but clearly emphasizes that we must begin with prayer, asking the Holy Spirit to guide our study—otherwise, it will just be an empty method.

1. *Observation:* In observation, we must ask questions of the text. Ask the who, what, when, where, how, and why of the text. Do your investigative work. Observation helps you understand what the text is saying.

2. *Interpretation:* Interpretation should help you understand what it means. This is where an understanding of the times and culture is paramount.

3. *Application:* Application seeks to help you understand how to apply what it means to your life in practice. About what is the Holy Spirit convicting you as you read the text?

---

[3] Precept Ministries International, "Inductive Bible Study," accessed March 7, 2023, https://www.moodychurch.org/wp-content/uploads/2018/01/Precepts-Precept-Ministries-Inductive-Study-Overview.pdf.

What heart change is necessary? What action must you take? These are all questions that must be answered in the application step of the study method; otherwise, transformation will not occur.

I encourage every Bible teacher to use the Inductive Bible study method.

Responsibility Six: Use the proper tools to rightly divide the Word of Truth.

Paul gave Timothy another piece of advice concerning Bible study. He said, "All Scripture is God-breathed and is useful for *teaching, rebuking, correcting and training in righteousness,* so that the servant of God may be *thoroughly equipped* for every good work" (2 Timothy 3:16-17 NIV). This Scripture highlights the last responsibility I want to discuss—continue to equip yourself.

The Bible teacher needs "thorough" equipping, which includes teaching, rebuking, correcting, and training. As teachers, we must be teachable, rebukeable, correctable, and trainable. When the Bible teacher thinks they no longer need to be taught, danger awaits them. When we think we no longer need training, we are on the brink of growing stale. Keep improving, being corrected, rebuked, and trained.

The equipper must continue to be equipped. That also means continuing to add tangible teaching skills to the teaching grace with which God has endowed you. Learn about adult learning principles, teaching technologies, public speaking, etc. Improve and hone what God has given you—seek out equipping. Seek to excel at teaching, not merely get by. There is a difference between a raw gift and one that has been refined by continuous upgrading and skill. A dull knife may still cut, but people will pay extra for a professional, sharp one.

Responsibility Seven: Seek to excel at teaching (not merely getting by) by continuous equipping.

As a Bible teacher, I have made it a personal goal to keep these responsibilities at the forefront of my heart and mind; I invite you to do the same. Cultivating the heart and spirit attitudes they reflect will help ensure longevity in the teaching ministry and give room for the Lord to always be glorified by our teaching.

Now, take a moment to review this chapter's key points. Then, reflect individually or discuss the questions with other Bible teachers.

Chapter Key Points

- *Responsibility One: Be a doer of what you teach.* (James 2:26-3:1)
- *Responsibility Two: Come up higher, repent quicker, and change faster than others. Cultivate repentance as a lifestyle.* (Luke 12:47-48)
- *Responsibility Three: Let the Word of God transform you first. Focus on continual transformation to avoid self-deception.* (Romans 12:2)
- *Responsibility Four: Be mature in your words. Discipline your tongue, mature in your word choices, and develop your vocabulary.* (John 6:63, Matthew 12:34)
- *Responsibility Five: Before you present your teaching to men, present yourself to God. Focus on pleasing him, not impressing men.* (2 Timothy 2:15)
- *Responsibility Six: Use the proper tools to rightly divide the Word of Truth.* (2 Timothy 2:15)
- *Responsibility Seven: Seek to excel at teaching (not merely getting by) by continuous equipping.* (2 Timothy 3:16-17)

Reflect or Discuss

1. Based on the Scriptures and insights shared in this chapter, can anyone be a Bible teacher? Why?

2. Which responsibility stuck with you the most or stood out most? Why?

3. Are you ready to accept these seven responsibilities, and why? If you have any hesitation, reflect or discuss why you think the hesitation is present?

4. Do you have the basic tools listed to study the Bible and correctly handle the Word of Truth?

5. What questions, if any, do you have about the Inductive Bible study method? What has been your experience putting it into practice?

In the next chapter, we discuss the goal of the teaching ministry by looking at Jesus' ultimate teaching goal. We'll explore questions like: Why am I even doing this? What's the point? What should be my focus? Who is really the central focus of my teaching? Let's continue.

Chapter 3

The Goal of the Teaching Ministry

---

*Now I saw heaven opened, and behold, a white horse.
And He who sat on him was called Faithful and
True, and in righteousness He judges and makes
war. ¹² His eyes were like a flame of fire, and on His
head were many crowns. He had a name written that
no one knew except Himself. ¹³ He was clothed with a
robe dipped in blood, and His name is called The
Word of God. ¹⁸ No one has seen God at any
time. The only begotten Son, who is in the bosom of the
Father, He has declared Him. (Revelation 19:11-13,
18 NKJV, italics added)*

Myles Munroe said, "When purpose is unknown, abuse is inevitable." Every Bible teacher must evaluate their goals and motives for teaching and ensure they understand the purpose of the teaching ministry from Christ's perspective. Take a moment and consider why you teach or want to teach. What's the point? Why are you even doing this? Who is really the central focus of your teaching, and what should be your focus?

Proverbs 4:7b says, "And in all your getting, get understanding." As Bible teachers, it is important for us to understand why we are doing what we do. We can't only focus on "the how" of teaching. We need to evaluate our "why."

To understand the purpose of the teaching ministry and evaluate our "why," we must turn first to Jesus as our example and ask, why did Jesus teach? There are many things the Savior could have been known for, including prophecy, evangelism, or church planting. But he chose to spend most of his time teaching. He was known popularly as "Rabbi," which means "my teacher" or "my master" in Hebrew. A rabbi was a master teacher with a following of pupils or disciples.

Why did Jesus teach?

The law and the prophets were until John. Since that time the kingdom of God has been preached, and everyone is pressing into it. (Luke 16:16 NKJV)

Jesus taught because he came to introduce a new way of living—a new kingdom. That kingdom directly opposed the Jews' thinking and understanding of what the promised messiah would do. They thought their messiah would use military force to deal with the Roman oppression and occupation of their land. But Jesus came riding on a humble donkey and teaching a strange new concept called the Gospel of the Kingdom. It was not what they expected, and for them to understand the new kingdom he represented and the God who sent him, Jesus needed to teach.

When he saw how far they were from understanding the Kingdom that had been prepared for them, he was moved with compassion, and according to the passage in Mark 6:34, compassion motivated him to teach.

And Jesus, when He came out, saw a great multitude and *was moved with compassion for them,* because they were like sheep not having a shepherd. So He *began to teach them many things.* (Mark 6:34 NKJV, italics added)

Does compassion motivate your teaching?

Teaching brings understanding, and both his disciples and the masses lacked understanding of the Kingdom of God. That was Jesus' main reason for teaching. He desperately wanted to reveal the Father's heart and kingdom to his people. This should also be the motive and focus of our teaching ministries—compassion to reveal the Father and his kingdom through Christ. It is through Christ that God has revealed his thoughts, intent, and desires for his people. According to Hebrews 11:2, God, in these last days, is speaking to us by his Son.

> God, who at various times and in various ways spoke in time past to the fathers by the prophets, 2 has in these last days spoken to us by His Son, whom He has appointed heir of all things, through whom also He made the worlds; 3 who being the brightness of His glory and the express image of His person, and upholding all things by the word of His power, when He had by Himself purged our sins, sat down at the right hand of the Majesty on high. (Hebrews 1:1-3 NKJV)

What does it mean for God to speak to us through his Son? His Son is the expressed image of himself. Words are thoughts articulated in human language. Jesus is God articulated in human flesh. If the disciples and masses wanted to know what God was like, they had only to listen to Jesus and observe the Father in him. Consider how the following passages from the book of John communicate that truth:

> In the beginning was the Word, and the Word was with God, and the Word was God. 2 He was in the beginning with God. 3 All things were made through Him, and without Him nothing was made that was made. 4 In Him was life, and the life was the light of men. 5 And the light

shines in the darkness, and the darkness did
not comprehend it. (John 1:1-5 NKJV)

Then Jesus answered and said to them, "Most assuredly, I
say to you, the Son can do nothing of Himself, but what
He sees the Father do; for whatever He does, the Son also
does in like manner. (John 5:19 NKJV)

. . . but these are written that you may believe that Jesus is
the Christ, the Son of God, and that believing you may
have life in His name. (John 20:31 NKJV)

For I have given to them the words which You have given
Me; and they have received *them,* and have known surely
that I came forth from You; and they have believed
that You sent Me. (John 17:8 NKJV)

The focus of Jesus' teaching ministry was to reveal the Father. He
said, "I have given them the words which You have given me."
He was not teaching for self-promotion. He was teaching to reveal
the Father who sent him. That is what our teaching should also
do. It should bring its hearers closer to God. It should bring an
understanding of the heart of the Father through Jesus. Our
teaching should promote and reveal Jesus—not ourselves. It
should be communicated with a like motive to Jesus' and in the
same Spirit in which Jesus taught.

Without the compassion of Jesus, our teaching will be routine,
robotic, puffed up, and without passion and effect. The hallmarks
of Jesus' ministry were teaching and healing because he had
compassion. Compassion drove him to both teach and heal. Why?
He was moved to demonstrate the new kingdom he was teaching
about, and the way he did that was to heal after he taught.
Compassion created holistic ministry. He taught them to liberate
their minds (souls) and spirits, and he healed them to liberate their
bodies. This is the compassion of Christ.

> And Jesus went about all Galilee, teaching in their synagogues, preaching the gospel of the kingdom, and healing all kinds of sickness and all kinds of disease among the people. (Matthew 4:23 NKJV)

The Legacy Must Continue

After Jesus gave his disciples the Great Commission and ascended back to the Father, they continued to teach and preach in the same motive and Spirit as their rabbi had. According to Acts 5:42 NKJV, "And daily in the temple, and in every house, they did not cease teaching and preaching Jesus *as* the Christ." We must continue the teaching legacy of Jesus and his disciples—in motive and Spirit. Note what the Scripture says about the apostles' teaching.

> Now when they saw the boldness of Peter and John, and perceived that they were uneducated and untrained men, they marveled. And they realized that they had been with Jesus. (Acts 4:13 NKJV)

> For it is the God who commanded light to shine out of darkness, who has shone in our hearts to give the light of the knowledge of the glory of God in the face of Jesus Christ. 7 But we have this treasure in earthen vessels, that the excellence of the power may be of God and not of us. (2 Corinthians 4:6-7 NKJV)

Peter and John were uneducated and untrained. Still, they taught with boldness and declared there was an excellency of power in what they were doing. My mother always said, "If you're 'gonna do something, do it well." The apostles may not have had education, but they still had excellence because they looked to Jesus as the power source of their teaching. The time they spent in his presence was noticeable when they taught. Is it noticeable when you teach?

Are you seeking to excel in your teaching ministry? Are you walking in excellence in your teaching? Excelling means you are adding skill to the raw teaching grace God gave you *and* cultivating the anointing that comes from his presence. You need both. Take note of the following Scriptures about excellence:

> Even so ye, forasmuch as ye are zealous of spiritual gifts, seek that ye may *excel* to the edifying of the church. (1 Corinthians 14:12 KJV, italics added)

> But we have this treasure in earthen vessels, that *the excellency of the power* may be of God, and not of us. (2 Corinthians 4:7 KJV, italics added)

> Yea doubtless, and I count all things but loss *for the excellency of the knowledge of Christ Jesus* my Lord: for whom I have suffered the loss of all things, and do count them but dung, that I may win Christ. (Philippians 3:8 KJV, italics added)

Merriam-Webster's Dictionary defines excellence as the quality of being superior, first-class, or the very best of its kind.[4] Every Bible teacher should seek to excel in their teaching. They should desire and put effort toward their teaching being the very best of its kind. And the best kind of teaching employs both skill and anointing to point people to the Father's heart through the person of Jesus Christ. Let's seek to excel in the edifying of the Church. Let Christ be our goal.

---

[4] Merriam-Webster Online Dictionary, s.v. "excellent," https://www.merriam-webster.com/dictionary/excellent (accessed March 8, 2023).

Take a moment to review this chapter's key points. Then, reflect individually or discuss the questions with a group of Bible teachers.

Chapter Key Points

- Myles Munroe said, "When purpose is unknown, abuse is inevitable." We must understand our motives for teaching and the purpose of the teaching ministry in the Church.
- We can't only focus on "the how" of teaching. We need to evaluate our "why."
- Jesus could have been known as a prophet or church planter, but he chose to spend much time teaching. For people to understand the new kingdom he represented and the God who sent him, Jesus needed to teach.
- When he saw how far the people were from understanding the kingdom that had been prepared for them, he was moved with compassion, and according to the passage in Mark 6:34, compassion motivated him to teach.
- The focus of Jesus' teaching ministry was to reveal the Father. He said, "I have given them the words which You have given me." He was not teaching for self-promotion.
- Without the compassion of Jesus, our teaching will be routine, robotic, puffed up, and without passion and effect.
- We must continue the teaching legacy of Jesus and his disciples—in motive and Spirit.
- The best kind of teaching employs both skill and anointing to point people to the Father's heart through the person of Jesus Christ. Let's seek to excel in the edifying of the Church.

Reflect or Discuss

1. In your own words, what is the teaching ministry, and what is its purpose? Explain.

2. Why and what did Jesus teach?

3. Does compassion motivate your teaching? Explain.

4. What does it mean for God to speak to us through his Son?

5. In this chapter, we stated, "The best kind of teaching employs both skill and anointing." In your own words, what does this statement mean?

In the next chapter, we explore the concept of Christian Education and its unique characteristics and learning environments.

Chapter 4

What is Christian Education?

*Having the right goal is essential for Christian
education to be effective.* — *Neil T. Anderson*

*The key distinctive of a truly Christian education ... is
the effective practice of worldview integration, that is, an
approach to biblical integration that leads to a
Christian worldview.* — *Martha MacCullough*

When you hear the word education, what comes to
mind? Do you think about your elementary school
days, going to college, or envision a student raising
their hand in a classroom? Most people who grew up in a Western
society associate education with a physical school or campus.
However, *Christian Education* happens mostly in settings and
contexts other than a school building—especially in America,
where prayer and Christian education are no longer incorporated
into public schools. Indeed, Christian Education is something
different from secular education, and its uniqueness must be
considered by the Bible teacher.

Christian Education can happen in homes through
homeschooling, small groups, and family Bible studies and

devotions. It can occur in a church building during adult or children's Sunday School, women's or men's fellowship, youth meetings, or primary services. It can also happen in private Christian schools, Christian universities, public coffee shops and restaurants, on Zoom, or on social media. And it's not always segmented by age or gender. Unlike secular schools, the Christian educator or Bible teacher is often challenged to teach a single set of content to an audience that includes people of various levels of spiritual maturity, ages, genders, reading levels, educational levels, cultures, learning styles, and socio-economic backgrounds. The Bible teacher must consider all these elements of their audience. So, Christian Education is unique and presents a unique set of challenges to the Bible teacher.

While it has been said that secular education focuses primarily on academic and vocational preparation for future living and working, Christian Education focuses on spiritual and Biblical preparation for victorious Christian living, discipleship, and faith-sharing (evangelism). Christian Education means that Christ and his Kingdom's Worldview are central to the education offered. Secular education propagates several humanistic worldviews—this should not be so with Christian education. While various worldviews can be critically examined, Christian Education should have the Kingdom Worldview woven into its fabric because Kingdom is what Jesus taught, and it is the reality every Christian should simultaneously live in, advance, and await its fullness.

With this in mind, it is essential that every Bible teacher understand what Kingdom Worldview means. Generally, a worldview is a comprehensive conception, apprehension, set of assumptions, or philosophy of the universe and humanity's relation to it from a specific standpoint.[5] So Kingdom Worldview is a philosophy of the universe and humanity from the standpoint of God as King of all Kings and sovereign ruler of his kingdom.

Four important truths frame the Kingdom Worldview: Creation, the Fall, Redemption, and Transformation.

> **Creation:** According to Genesis, God extended his heavenly kingdom to earth during Creation. He made man and woman in his image, and he gave man and woman dominion over the extension of his kingdom—the earth. Earth was to be one of his domains, with man and woman as his delegated authority to tend it.
>
>> Then God said, "Let Us make man in Our image, according to Our likeness; let them have dominion over the fish of the sea, over the birds of the air, and over the cattle, over all the earth and over every creeping thing that creeps on the earth." [27] So God created man in His own image; in the image of God He created him; male and female He created them. [28] Then God blessed them, and God said to them, "Be fruitful and multiply; fill the earth and subdue it; have dominion over the fish of the sea, over the birds of the air, and over every living thing that moves on the earth." (Genesis 1:26-28 NKJV)

Fall: Man and woman fell prey to the serpent's enticement to sin in the Garden, losing the dominion God gave them. They seeded their dominion mandate to the devil through sin. That is why when the devil tempted

---

[5] Dictionary.com, s.v. "worldview," https://www.dictionary.com/browse/worldview (accessed March 8, 2023).

Jesus in the wilderness, he could boldly say the kingdoms of the world had been delivered to him. See the passages in Genesis and Luke below.

> And the LORD God said to the woman, "What *is* this you have done?" The woman said, "The serpent deceived me, and I ate." **14** So the LORD God said to the serpent: "Because you have done this, You *are* cursed more than all cattle, And more than every beast of the field; On your belly you shall go, And you shall eat dust All the days of your life. **15** And I will put enmity Between you and the woman, And between your seed and her Seed; He shall bruise your head, And you shall bruise His heel." **16** To the woman He said: "I will greatly multiply your sorrow and your conception; In pain you shall bring forth children; Your desire *shall be* for your husband, And he shall rule over you." **17** Then to Adam He said, "Because you have heeded the voice of your wife, and have eaten from the tree of which I commanded you, saying, 'You shall not eat of it': "Cursed *is* the ground for your sake; In toil you shall eat *of* it All the days of your life. **18** Both thorns and thistles it shall bring forth for you, And you shall eat the herb of the field. **19** In the sweat of your face you shall eat bread Till you return to the ground, For out of it you were taken; For dust you *are,* And to dust you shall return." (Genesis 3:13-19 NKJV)

> Then the devil, taking Him up on a high mountain, showed Him all the kingdoms of the world in a moment of time. **6** And the devil said to

Him, "All this authority I will give You, and their glory; for this has been delivered to me, and I give it to whomever I wish. (Luke 4:5-6 NKJV)

Redemption: Even amid the fall, God had a plan for redemption (see Genesis 3:15 below). Jesus came to earth to destroy the devil's works (1 John 3:8b) and redeem us from the fall. In the process, he restored dominion back to man and woman (John 14:12).

And I will put enmity Between you and the woman, And between your seed and her Seed; He shall bruise your head, And you shall bruise His heel." (Genesis 3:15 NKJV)

. . . For this purpose the Son of God was manifested, that He might destroy the works of the devil. (1 John 3:8b NKJV)

"Most assuredly, I say to you, he who believes in Me, the works that I do he will do also; and greater works than these he will do, because I go to My Father. (John 14:12 NKJV)

Transformation: Now, through his name—the name of Jesus—redeemed men and woman can take back dominion from the enemy (Luke 11:20, Mark 16:17-18) and enforce "his kingdom come" on earth as it is in heaven (Luke 11:2). We don't have to conform to the world system, or adopt a secular worldview; we can transform it (Romans 12:2, 2 Corinthians 3:18, 2 Corinthians 11:15). Moreover, we will ultimately be transformed and conformed to Jesus' glorious body and image (Philippians 3:21).

But if I cast out demons with the finger of God, surely the kingdom of God has come upon you. (Luke 11:20 NKJV)

And these signs will follow those who believe: In My name they will cast out demons; they will speak with new tongues; [18] they will take up serpents; and if they drink anything deadly, it will by no means hurt them; they will lay hands on the sick, and they will recover." (Mark 16:17-18 NKJV)

And he said unto them, When ye pray, say, Our Father which art in heaven, Hallowed be thy name. Thy kingdom come. Thy will be done, as in heaven, so in earth. (Luke 11:2 NKJV)

And do not be conformed to this world, but be transformed by the renewing of your mind, that you may prove what is that good and acceptable and perfect will of God. (Romans 12:2 NKJV)

But we all, with unveiled face, beholding as in a mirror the glory of the Lord, are being transformed into the same image from glory to glory, just as by the Spirit of the Lord. (2 Corinthians 3:18 NKJV)

Therefore it is no great thing if his ministers also transform themselves into ministers of righteousness, whose end will be according to their works. (2 Corinthians 11:15 NKJV)

who will transform our lowly body that it may be
conformed to His glorious body, according to the
working by which He is able even to subdue all
things to Himself. (Philippians 3:21 NKJV)

These critical truths of Kingdom Worldview should affect how we
teach the Bible. We are not sharing information for the sake of
knowledge alone but to prepare Believers for the establishment of
God's Kingdom and to aid the process of transformation. Secular
education may focus on academic preparation or preparation to
enter the labor force. However, Christian Education must focus
on preparing a people to:

- Know their Creator!
- Overcome the wiles of the enemy, so they don't fall like
  Adam and Eve.
- Redeem the earth by exercising their dominion mandate.
- Be transformed and conformed to the image of Christ.

This type of Christian Education reflects a Kingdom Worldview,
which sets its students up for Kingdom success. So, Bible
teachers, let's fully embrace a Kingdom Worldview and the true
meaning of Christian Education!

Take a moment to review this chapter's key points. Then, reflect
individually or discuss the questions with a group of Bible
teachers.

Chapter Key Points

- Unlike secular schools, the Christian educator or Bible
  teacher is often challenged to teach a single set of content
  to an audience that includes people of various levels of
  spiritual maturity, ages, genders, reading levels,
  educational levels, cultures, learning styles, and socio-

economic backgrounds. The Bible teacher must consider all these elements of their audience.

- Christian Education focuses on spiritual and biblical preparation for victorious Christian living, discipleship, and faith-sharing (evangelism). Christian Education means that Christ and his Kingdom's Worldview are central to the education offered.

- Kingdom Worldview is a philosophy of the universe and humanity from the standpoint of God as King of all Kings and sovereign ruler of his kingdom.

- Four important truths frame the Kingdom Worldview: Creation, the Fall, Redemption, and Transformation.

- These critical truths of Kingdom Worldview should affect how we teach the Bible. We are not sharing information for the sake of knowledge alone but to prepare Believers for the establishment of God's Kingdom and to aid the process of transformation.

- Christian Education must focus on preparing a people to:
  o Know their Creator!
  o Overcome the wiles of the enemy, so they don't fall like Adam and Eve.
  o Redeem the earth by exercising their dominion mandate.
  o Be transformed and conformed to the image of Christ.

Reflect or Discuss

1. How can the Bible teacher accommodate an audience that includes people of various levels of spiritual maturity, ages, genders, reading levels, educational levels, cultures, learning styles, and socio-economic backgrounds? Explain.

2. How is Christian Education different from secular education?

3. Explain the Kingdom Worldview and how should it affect your teaching ministry?

4. What should be the focus of Christian Education? Why?

In the next chapter, we focus on teaching adults and discuss key principles of adult learning. We'll answer questions like: Why does it matter that my audience is adults? How do I address the fact that adults have varying learning styles, educational levels, and cultural backgrounds?

Chapter 5

Understanding How Adults Learn

---

*The Biblical educator must not only have a Christian
understanding of the material, he must have a Biblical
understanding of the student. If he does not, then the
result will be a hybrid Christian methodology employed
to achieve a humanistic goal. — Douglas Wilson*

I f you don't understand your student, you limit the
effectiveness of your teaching. You may occasionally "hit the
mark" and help your student learn something. But if you
know your audience well and design instruction for their unique
characteristics, you will consistently facilitate compelling learning
experiences. If you teach adults, you must understand the unique
aspects of how adults learn.

> *If you don't understand your student, you limit the
> effectiveness of your teaching.*

We must emphasize this—the way adults learn is different from
children. For example, a child may automatically see you as an
authority figure because you are the teacher and older, but an
adult will not. Children will undergo certain brain development
stages that adults have already encountered. Moreover, children
do not have real-life experiences—adults do. They are not

children. This is the basis for the term andragogy, coined by educator Malcolm Knowles in the 1980s. Andragogy is the practice of teaching adults, while pedagogy is the practice of teaching children. The two things are different animals altogether.

Perhaps you've had an experience where someone tried to teach you like you were a child. This often happens when someone has been faithful as a children's ministry teacher and then gets "promoted" to teaching adult Sunday school. Unfortunately, they often fail to make the necessary shift because they are unaware of adult learning principles. If you've encountered this, I'm sure it was a less-than-effective and possibly even insulting experience. Perhaps they assumed you knew nothing and approached the information at a most basic level, reading to you word for word from slides without any additional information. Maybe they never asked you to contribute to the discussion? Whatever the case, when adult instruction is not approached correctly, learning diminishes. For this reason, the Bible teacher of adults needs to explore the critical principles of adult learning and apply them to their teaching ministry.

Five Principles of Teaching Adults

There are entire university degree programs and lengthy courses devoted to andragogy and adult learning principles. Of course, we cannot exhaust them all, but there are five that I have found essential for the Bible teacher to discuss.

Principle One: Make Sure Your Adult Students Understand "Why"

Adults have limited time, busy schedules, and ever-diminishing attention spans. The worst mistake you can make as a Bible teacher is to think everyone in your adult audience is ready to take you seriously. You must convince them to listen to you, or they will quickly "tune you out." They must understand why what you say is relevant and important for them to know. There is a need to explain why specific things are being taught and convince them to attend to what you have to say.

The other reality is that age, life experience, and habits formed over time can lead adults to be "set in their ways." This is an enemy of openness to learning. That means while you are teaching, an adult who has come to accept a different perspective could be fighting with you in their mind the entire time. Therefore, Bible teachers need to explain why learners need to listen and why they must change their way of thinking. They should also help adult learners to understand new concepts in relation to old ones by comparison, contrast, pros, and cons.

Principle Two: Respect that Your Students Have Different Educational Backgrounds and Learning Styles

Instruction should consider that adults have various educational levels, cultural backgrounds, and learning styles. Therefore, learning materials and activities should be varied, considering learners' previous experiences, and addressing different learning styles.

When designing instruction for varying educational levels, key things to consider are vocabulary and reading levels. This means that using the King James Version of the Bible will be difficult for those who did not complete High School or whose cultural backgrounds do not lend themselves to such language. Choose your Bible versions well. You can create a brief, five-question student questionnaire to assess everyone's educational level and discover any concerns they have (see Appendix B).

Be aware that some may be hesitant to read the Bible out loud in class because they have a low reading ability and don't want to be embarrassed. This means that in addition to asking someone to read, you can also ask someone to summarize what another person read and tell you, in their own words, what the Scriptures meant.

Illustrations and examples should not be from one culture. Instead, use varied cultural examples and language to clarify key points.

Learning styles mean that some people comprehend better by seeing a visual while others comprehend best by listening or doing/experimenting. There are several theories of learning styles. However, the basic theory is that there are three primary learning styles:

- **Visual:** Visual learners best learn new information with their eyes. They need charts, diagrams, pictures, and symbols. They cannot sit and listen to you for minutes and hours on end without any visual stimulation. You may see drawings and symbols on their note-taking pages. They will refrain from paying attention to you, and they will not retain what they hear you say if don't use visuals.

- **Auditory:** Auditory learners best absorb new information by listening. They thrive on lectures, discussion groups, and audio recordings, for example, podcasts. They need to read aloud and discuss concepts with others to solidify learning. They want to hear how the Bible teacher will explain new information. These people will go back and listen to recorded messages—even if they are audio-only.

- **Kinesthetic:** Kinesthetic learners best absorb new information by doing. Their learning thrives when they can use all their senses in the learning experience, including sight, touch, taste, smell, and hearing. They want to engage with the learning experience, practice, and experience it. Tutorials, labs, and practice demonstrations that allow the learner to participate best help this type of learner.

The best learning experiences incorporate elements that address all three learning styles. There will be visual aids to accompany lectures and time for practice activities and discussion. Adult learners should only sit and listen part of the time. They need to engage the material. Moreover, with the onset of so many Zoom meetings, visuals, sound effects, and break-out activities have become increasingly important to effective learning. When teaching online Bible studies, varying the learning experience to break up the monotony of so many online meetings is essential to retaining learners' attention.

Principle Three: Use Your Students' Experience as a Resource

Let students share their life experiences to enrich learning and solidify key points. Instead of having a student who frequently interrupts your lecture to prove they know everything, allow them and others to share experiences to drive home the consequences and benefits of certain actions or behaviors. Some adults will have more experience than others, but through discussion, everyone can benefit. When students from different walks of life share their experiences, everyone gains new and useful perspectives.

Tap into the life experiences of your students, especially when discussing how to apply the Scriptures to daily life. Discussing how to apply the Bible teaching to life is essential to help students be doers of the Word and not hearers only. When students discuss their life experiences, it can help others gain ideas for applying the Word of God to their daily lives.

The downside of sharing life experience is that adults can try to validate new information you give them with past experiences before fully accepting what you say. That might create resistance. They may also think they know more than they do. Use discussion to address this and bring in alternative perspectives. Also, keep in mind that you may have to emphasize Jesus' life experiences and counsel as superior to their life experience.

Principle Four: When the Student Is Ready, the Teacher Appears

Adults who choose to come early for Sunday school, stay late for special topic classes, or attend teachings outside of regular church service times are usually self-motivated to learn. They would have made a choice to pursue more biblical knowledge. In this case, the Bible teacher's role is to encourage that internal motivation and not squelch it. They should help their students remain positive and move past any apprehension they feel about learning. In addition, they should not disappoint this motivation with mediocre preparation and lackluster materials. Adults who are motivated to learn will quickly go somewhere else if they feel their time and motivation are being wasted. This is, in part, why excellence and preparation are necessary.

Principle Five: Encourage Your Adult Students

Encouragement is key. Sometimes, a Bible teacher must be a coach, cheering their students on to learn. Older students may need encouragement to overcome apprehension about using technology. Others may need encouragement because they never finished High school or are apprehensive about learning because the academic habits they had perished long ago. Create an encouraging learning environment and communicate things at varying educational levels. Explain terms that learners with less education may not know. Don't attack learners when they mispronounce words. Encourage them. Reassure them. Cheer for them.

When applied, these five adult learning principles will elevate your teaching ministry and provide more effective learning experiences for your Bible students.

Take a moment to review this chapter's key points. Then, reflect individually or discuss the questions with other Bible teachers.

Chapter Key Points

- If you don't understand your student, you limit the effectiveness of your teaching.
- The way adults learn is different from the way children learn. Don't teach adults like you are teaching children.
- Adults must understand why what you have to say is relevant and important for them to know. There is a need to explain the reasons specific things are being taught and convince them that they need to attend to what you have to say.
- The basic theory of learning styles is that there are three primary learning styles: visual, auditory, and kinesthetic.
- With the onset of so many Zoom meetings, visuals, sound effects, and break-out activities have become increasingly important to effective learning.
- Let students share their life experiences to enrich learning and solidify key points.
- The Bible teacher's role is to encourage a learner's internal motivation and not squelch it.

- Create an encouraging learning environment and communicate things at varying educational levels. Help learners overcome apprehension.

Reflect or Discuss

1. Why is it important to know your learners' characteristics, e.g., their educational background, culture, and learning style? How can you discover this information?

2. How can you address all their learning styles—visual, auditory, and kinesthetic—in your Bible teaching? Explain and give examples for each style.

3. How can you make Zoom teaching sessions more engaging?

4. How can you encourage learner motivation and not quench it?

In the next chapter, we examine Jesus' teaching methods and approaches. We'll analyze why there is no one greater than Jesus, after which to model our teaching ministry.

Chapter 6

Jesus, the Master Teacher: Methods of Teaching

Jesus is a teacher who doesn't just inform our intellect but forms our very loves. He isn't content to simply deposit new ideas into your mind; he is after nothing less than your wants, your loves, your longings. —
James K.A. Smith

When we label someone a master, it means they exhibit the utmost skill and talent at doing something and are a model others should follow and emulate. Other names for a master include expert, chief, or principal. Masters often have the responsibility of teaching and mentoring others. So, in this chapter, we take Jesus as our Master Teacher and teaching ministry mentor to examine the hallmarks of his teaching ministry. If anyone was a master, expert, chief, or principal teacher, it was Jesus. Let's examine the evidence for this thesis or assertion.

Jesus' teaching ministry was not limited by location or setting. He taught on mountains, in boats, synagogues, temples, villages, homes, and more. His audience sizes ranged from a few to thousands. Think about it.

He never had notes and an outline on physical paper. We only saw him using physical paper to teach when he took the scroll in the temple to read. He could adjust to almost any teaching situation and setting. Somehow, he managed to pull it off. The varying environments didn't shake his focus. He could deliver his teaching almost anywhere.

He never used a microphone, megaphone, or electronic sound system—even when he preached to thousands. Instead, his disciples helped to echo his message, and his listeners were captivated, giving him their full attention. The Scripture tells us that Eutychus fell asleep as Paul was preaching (Acts 20:9), but this kind of thing is never recorded during Jesus' teaching.

Jesus taught people from various cultures. He taught Romans, Samaritans, Jews, Syrophoenicians, Canaanites, and more. Jews and Gentiles alike felt a commonality with his illustrations, stories, and examples. Somehow, Jesus could teach in a way that multiple cultures could relate, maintain interest, and be convinced of the truth of his message.

Jesus taught people of varying educational levels. The Scriptures note that Peter and John were unlearned, uneducated men (Acts 4:13). They never obtained higher levels of education—they were fishermen by trade. Still, Jesus, a tradesman himself—a carpenter—also taught the educated Pharisees, Scribes, and teachers of the law. Thinking themselves wise, they often tried to trap him with questions, but he put them to shame with the wisdom in his teaching.

If that's not enough to convince us that Jesus was a master teacher, there's more. He often varied his teaching approach and methods for the audience he addressed. For example, consider the passage in Mark 4.

> And again He began to teach by the sea. And a great
> multitude was gathered to Him, so that He got into a boat

and sat in it on the sea; and the whole multitude was on the land facing the sea. 2 Then He taught them many things by parables, and said to them in His teaching: 3 "Listen! Behold, a sower went out to sow. 4 And it happened, as he sowed, that some seed fell by the wayside; and the birds of the air came and devoured it. 5 Some fell on stony ground, where it did not have much earth; and immediately it sprang up because it had no depth of earth. 6 But when the sun was up it was scorched, and because it had no root it withered away. 7 And some seed fell among thorns; and the thorns grew up and choked it, and it yielded no crop. 8 But other seed fell on good ground and yielded a crop that sprang up, increased and produced: some thirtyfold, some sixty, and some a hundred." 9 And He said to them, "He who has ears to hear, let him hear!" 10 But when He was alone, those around Him with the twelve asked Him about the parable. 11 And He said to them, "To you it has been given to know the mystery of the kingdom of God; but to those who are outside, all things come in parables, 12 so that 'Seeing they may see and not perceive, And hearing they may hear and not understand; Lest they should turn, And their sins be forgiven them.' " 13 And He said to them, "Do you not understand this parable? How then will you understand all the parables? 14 The sower sows the word. 15 And these are the ones by the wayside where the word is sown. When they hear, Satan comes immediately and takes away the word that was sown in their hearts. 16 These likewise are the ones sown on stony ground who, when they hear the word, immediately receive it with gladness; 17 and they have no root in themselves, and so endure only for a time. Afterward, when tribulation or persecution arises for the word's sake, immediately they stumble. [18] Now these are the ones sown among thorns; they are the ones who hear the word, [19] and the cares of this world, the deceitfulness of riches, and the desires for other things entering in choke the word, and it becomes unfruitful. [20] But these are the ones sown on good ground, those who hear the word, accept it, and bear fruit: some thirtyfold, some sixty, and some a hundred." (Mark 4:1-20 NKJV)

In this passage of Scripture, the setting is the seaside. Jesus is sitting in a boat teaching a multitude of people who are sitting on the seashore. The method of teaching he uses is parables. Parables are simple stories used to illustrate or teach spiritual lessons.[6] They use everyday life events or "once upon a time stories" to make comparisons to and illuminate spiritual realities. In this passage, the parable is not a real-life event but a story about a fictitious gardener that remains true to life. Jesus tells the story in a vivid, visual language that engages the learner.

Surprisingly, the twelve apostles and those with them did not understand Jesus' skillful presentation. They didn't get it. In response, Jesus explains to them that he used parables for a specific audience—those who are "outside." (Mark 4:11) But he told them their portion was to know the mysteries of the Kingdom, and understanding this parable was particularly necessary to understand all the others (Mark 4:13). Then, he explained the parable to them. Every Bible teacher must understand Jesus' explanation because, as the Bible teacher, you are the Sower.

---

[6] Dictionary.com, s.v., "parable,"
https://www.dictionary.com/browse/parable (accessed March 9, 2023).

The sower sows the word. ¹⁵ And these are the ones by the *wayside* where the word is sown. When they hear, Satan comes immediately and takes away the word that was sown in their hearts. ¹⁶ These likewise are the ones sown on *stony ground* who, when they hear the word, immediately receive it with gladness; ¹⁷ and they have no root in themselves, and so endure only for a time. Afterward, when tribulation or persecution arises for the word's sake, immediately they stumble. ¹⁸ Now these are the ones sown among *thorns*; they are the ones who hear the word, ¹⁹ and the cares of this world, the deceitfulness of riches, and the desires for other things entering in choke the word, and it becomes unfruitful. ²⁰ But these are the ones sown on *good ground*, those who hear the word, accept it, and bear fruit: some thirtyfold, some sixty, and some a hundred. (Mark 4:14-20 NKJV, italics added)

There are several things the Bible teacher must learn and remember from Jesus' explanation.

1. Your job is not to sow your opinions. It is to sow the Word of God.
2. Satan is in opposition to the sowing of the Word of God. He wants to snatch the very thing you are trying to impart—understanding.
3. There are always four groups of people listening to you:
    1) Wayside: They are there physically but not mentally. They are just there "by the way." Perhaps, they are in church because they want to find a girlfriend or boyfriend. The word is in one ear and out the other—Satan immediately takes away the word that is sown.
    2) Stony ground: Those with no root in themselves. They receive the teaching with gladness and even

shout while you teach, but that is all. The excitement leaves them before they even get to the classroom exit door. They stumble and can't hold on to what you have taught. It slips through their fingers before class is over.

3) Thorns: Those that receive the teaching, and hold onto it for a while until cares, concerns, and desires for other things choke the word out of them before they can bear fruit.

4) Good ground: Those whose hearts are good ground. These are the ones who hear the teaching, accept it, and bear fruit. This means the Bible teacher should be prepared for only one-fourth of their class to actually do something with what they teach.

Stop and think about that—one-fourth.

Now, let's look closer at Jesus' teaching methods and approaches.

Jesus' Teaching Methods and Approaches

Jesus taught with authority because he was under authority.

> The Jews there were amazed and asked, "How did this man get such learning without having been taught?" [16] Jesus answered, "My teaching is not my own. It comes from the one who sent me. [17] Anyone who chooses to do the will of God will find out whether my teaching comes from God or whether I speak on my own. (John 7:15-17 NIV)

You must be under authority to teach with authority. Please don't try to teach the Word of God and be a rebel. Stay submitted to your local leadership and be obedient to the Word of God you teach.

Jesus knew his audience.

> Immediately Jesus knew in his spirit that this was what they were thinking in their hearts, and he said to them, "Why are you thinking these things? (Mark 2:8 NIV)

You must know your audience to teach effectively. Jesus knew what was in the hearts of those he was teaching and adjusted his teaching method accordingly.

Jesus used parables and storytelling.

> Another parable He spoke to them: "The kingdom of heaven is like leaven, which a woman took and hid in three measures of meal till it was all leavened." (Matthew 13:33 NKJV)

People relate to stories. They love to follow characters, plot, setting, and scenery. Learn how to tell a good story to keep your audience engaged.

Jesus sometimes used language to shock people. He made sure he kept their attention.

> And if your right hand causes you to sin, cut it off and cast it from you; for it is more profitable for you that one of your members perish, than for your whole body to be cast into hell. (Matthew 5:30 NKJV)

A hyperbole is an exaggerated statement or claim not meant to be taken literally. Jesus used hyperbole to catch the attention of his learners and stress the importance of certain principles. Sometimes you need to shock your students to keep their attention or emphasize a point.

Jesus varied his teaching method for his audience when necessary.

> All these things Jesus spoke to the multitude in parables; and without a parable He did not speak to them. (Matthew 13:34 NKJV)

Jesus used parables for the multiple while explaining things in detail to those closer to him. He used Jewish examples when teaching Jews and other illustrations when interacting with Gentiles. When appropriate, adjust your teaching method for your audience. The focus is their learning not your preferences—this is the beginning of God-and-student-centered teaching.

Jesus asked questions. He engaged his learners in discussion.

> For what profit is it to a man if he gains the whole world, and loses his own soul? Or what will a man give in exchange for his soul? (Matthew 16:26 NKJV)

Jesus did not suffer his learners by restricting his teaching to lectures only. He used questions to provoke them to think and to confront their wrong attitudes.

Jesus used visuals and illustrations.

> At that time the disciples came to Jesus, saying, "Who then is greatest in the kingdom of heaven?" [2] Then Jesus called a little child to Him, set him in the midst of them, [3] and said, "Assuredly, I say to you, unless you are converted and become as little children, you will by no

means enter the kingdom of heaven. ⁴ Therefore whoever humbles himself as this little child is the greatest in the kingdom of heaven. (Matthew 18:1-4 NKJV)

After that, He poured water into a basin and began to wash the disciples' feet, and to wipe them with the towel with which He was girded. ¹² So when He had washed their feet, taken His garments, and sat down again, He said to them, "Do you know what I have done to you? ¹³ You call Me Teacher and Lord, and you say well, for so I am. ¹⁴ If I then, your Lord and Teacher, have washed your feet, you also ought to wash one another's feet. ¹⁵ For I have given you an example, that you should do as I have done to you. ¹⁶ Most assuredly, I say to you, a servant is not greater than his master; nor is he who is sent greater than he who sent him. ¹⁷ If you know these things, blessed are you if you do them. (John 13:5,12-17 NKJV)

Jesus may not have had PowerPoint, but he still used visuals. He demonstrated his servanthood message by washing his disciples' feet and then pointed out that his action was a lesson itself. He placed a child in front of the people he was teaching and then told them they had to have child-like faith to receive the kingdom fully. Jesus was a visual teacher.

Jesus used repetition.

For example, Jesus taught about this death and resurrection repeatedly (Mark 8:31, Mark 9:31, Mark 10:33–34). Yet his disciples seemingly could not understand it; Peter even rebuked him for teaching it. Never assume learners understand something because you said it once. Repeat your key points. Then repeat them again and again. It has been said that repetition is the mother of learning.

"Repetition is the mother of learning, the father of action, which makes it the architect of accomplishment." — Zig Ziglar

Jesus allowed his students to experience (practice) what he taught.

Jesus taught his disciples and then sent them out two by two to do what he taught them to do (Mark 6:7). In other words, he made them practice. He created tutorials, labs, and lived learning experiences for them to test and apply what they had learned. Your teaching must also provide opportunities to plan application of the Word of God, and practice it.

Indeed, Jesus is our Master Teacher. It cannot be denied. There is no one greater than Jesus after which to model your teaching ministry.

Take a moment to review this chapter's key points. Then, reflect individually or discuss the questions with other Bible teachers.

Chapter Key Points

- Jesus' teaching ministry was not limited by location or setting. He never used a microphone, megaphone, or electronic sound system—even when he preached to thousands.
- Jesus taught people from various cultures and educational levels.
- He often varied his teaching approach and methods for the audience he addressed.

- Every Bible teacher must understand Jesus' explanation of the Parable of the Sower because, as the Bible teacher, you are the Sower. There are several things the Bible teacher must learn and remember from Jesus' explanation.
  - Your job is not to sow your opinions. It is to sow the Word of God.
  - Satan is in opposition to the sowing of the Word of God. He wants to snatch the very thing you are trying to impart—understanding.
  - There are always four groups of people in your class:
    - Wayside: They are there physically but not mentally. They are just there "by the way." Perhaps, they are in church because they want to find a girlfriend or boyfriend. The word is in one ear and out the other—Satan immediately takes away the word that is sown.
    - Stony ground: Those with no root in themselves. They receive the teaching with gladness and even shout while you teach, but that is all. The excitement leaves them before they even get to the classroom exit door. They stumble and can't hold on to what you have taught. It slips through their fingers before class is over.
    - Thorns: Those that receive the teaching, and hold onto it for a while until cares, concerns, and desires for other things choke the word out of them before they can bear fruit.

- Good ground: Those whose hearts are good ground. These are the ones who hear the teaching, accept it, and bear fruit. This means the Bible teacher should be prepared for only one-fourth of their class to actually do something with what they teach.

- Jesus' teaching methods and approaches include but are not limited to the following list:
  o Jesus taught with authority because he was under authority.
  o Jesus knew his audience.
  o Jesus used parables and storytelling.
  o Jesus sometimes used language to shock people. He made sure he kept their attention.
  o Jesus varied his teaching method for his audience when necessary.
  o Jesus asked questions. He engaged his learners in discussion.
  o Jesus used visuals and illustrations.
  o Jesus used repetition.
  o Jesus allowed his students to experience (practice) what he taught.

Reflect or Discuss

1. Do you agree that Jesus was a Master Teacher? Explain.

2. What key lessons have you learned from the Parable of the Sower as it relates to your teaching ministry?

3. Should the one-fourth rule revealed in the Parable of the Sower discourage you or encourage you? Why?

4. Discuss three of Jesus' teaching methods and explain, in detail, how you will incorporate them into your teaching ministry. Why did these three catch your attention?

In the next chapter, you will thoroughly consider a God-and-student-centered approach to Bible teaching. Then, you will craft your personal teaching philosophy, explaining your reason and motivation for being a Bible teacher and the approach you will adopt for teaching the Bible to others.

Chapter 7

A God-and-Student-Centered Teaching Philosophy

They asked each other, "Were not our hearts burning within us while he talked with us on the road and opened the Scriptures to us?" (Luke 24:32 NIV)

According to Luke 24:32, the disciples' hearts burned as Jesus explained the Scriptures. Jesus' teaching ministry ignited a passion in their hearts. They wanted to hear more. They burned with passion for hearing more because his teaching opened their minds to a new level of revelation. Even though they were walking down a road with no physical Bible to look at, as he taught them, they "saw" something they had never seen before. Revelation happens when skillful, anointed Bible teaching helps the heart, the inner man, see something it has never seen before. That is what happened when Jesus taught. Does it happen when you teach? Regardless, it must remain every Bible teacher's goal.

The good news is if we heed the seven responsibilities of the Bible teacher discussed in Chapter 2, ensure our motives for teaching are in divine alignment, adopt a Kingdom Worldview, add adult learning principles to our teaching, and employ the teaching methods of Jesus, we should be well on our way to having the same kind of revelatory and transformative teaching ministry that Jesus had.

Two other crucial things we must understand are that Jesus' teaching ministry was both God-centered and student-centered.

God-Centered Teaching

Jesus said, "My teaching is not my own. It comes from the one who sent me" (John 7:16 NIV). He taught with authority because he stood in the authority of the one who sent him. When you teach, you must stand in the authority of Jesus, under the authority of your leader, and always remember your teaching ministry is not your own. What you say should come from the one who sent you. The next generation of great men and women of God don't need to hear your opinions—they need to hear the words of the Master. You must reflect the one who sent you and stay under the authority of the Scriptures you teach to be most effective when sharing them.

Jesus' teaching was God-centered. He didn't teach to seek his own glory but the glory of the Father who sent him. He further explained, "Whoever speaks on their own does so to gain personal glory, but he who seeks the glory of the one who sent him is a man of truth; there is nothing false about him" (John 7:18 NIV).

Be a Bible teacher of truth; let there be nothing false about you or your teaching. Adopt a God-centered teaching philosophy. And what we mean by philosophy is a set of principles to guide our teaching ministries.

Student-Centered Teaching

Jesus' teaching was also student-centered or learner-centered. He did not prioritize his preferences over what his students needed. Instead, his goal was to ensure those who really wanted could understand the Kingdom.

> And Jesus, when He came out, saw a great multitude and *was moved with compassion for them*, because they were like sheep not having a shepherd. So He began to teach them many things. (Mark 6:34 NKJV, italics added)

He was motivated by compassion for his students. That's the heart of student-centered teaching. You can tell when someone cares genuinely for their students.

You can also tell when a teacher tries to impress you and doesn't care whether you understand. It's all about them. They may be knowledgeable, but their knowledge has puffed up and become unattractive to everyone but them. The passage in Corinthians tells us, "Knowledge puffs up, but love edifies" (1 Corinthians 8:1). Let's commit to love and compassion in our teaching ministries. Let's adopt a student-centered teaching philosophy (principles to guide our teaching ministries).

Adopting a student-centered teaching philosophy means committing to empowering our students to achieve key Kingdom learning objectives or outcomes. Based on the four critical truths of the Kingdom Worldview from Chapter Four, Christian Education must focus on preparing a people to:

- Know their Creator!
- Overcome the enemy's wiles, so they don't fall like Adam and Eve.

- Redeem the earth by exercising their dominion mandate.
- Be transformed and conformed to the image of Christ.

This means our primary role as student-centered Bible teachers is to ensure that our students achieve these outcomes. The centrality of the Scriptures to our students' lives must be permanently fixed in our minds because understanding and applying the Scriptures will empower them to achieve Kingdom outcomes.

It is good practice for the Bible teacher to consistently reflect on whether their teaching is empowering their students to know God, overcome the enemy, take dominion, and be transformed into the image of Christ. There are other characteristics of student-centered learning.

Additional Characteristics of Student-Centered Learning:

- The focus is not on the instructor's delivery but on ensuring that students achieve their outcomes. The teacher is not the star but a facilitator of learning whose job is to understand their students and find appropriate means for their learning.
- The teacher(s) acts as both facilitator and member of the community of learners. The teacher's lesson/unit plans provide interaction options and accommodate various learning styles. The teacher guides practice on classroom procedures and activities.
- Multiple opportunities are provided for students to reflect. Student reflection is encouraged inside and outside of the classroom.
- Students can develop healthy relationships by praying for one another, doing group assignments outside of the classroom, or special events.

- Students are given ample resources to learn.

Your Personal Teaching Philosophy: What Kind of Teacher Do You Want to Be?

Every Bible teacher should articulate their teaching philosophy (the principles that guide their teaching ministry). Good practice dictates writing down the guiding principles that will direct you as you endeavor to fulfill your teaching ministry with excellence. Here are a few tips for writing your statement:

- It should describe what you believe about Bible teaching as it relates to your purpose and motives for being a Bible teacher.
- Articulate the objectives you are trying to achieve when teaching.
- Describe the methods you will use. Include concrete examples of what you will do in the classroom to support your purpose and beliefs. What methods will you employ?
- Describe the measures you will use to evaluate whether you remain true to your teaching purpose, values, and philosophy.

A well-written teaching philosophy statement is a means of intently evaluating your teaching approach for continuous improvement. It empowers you to communicate your teaching beliefs and values to your students, peers, and leaders. It is not set in stone. You should keep it and regularly revisit and update it as needed. Remember that Jesus' teaching was God-centered and student-centered. How might you incorporate those values in your statement?

Before you write your statement, take a moment to review this chapter's key points. Then, reflect individually or discuss the questions with other Bible teachers.

Note: This chapter includes an activity to help you write your teaching philosophy. Please do not skip it. Instead, write your one-page teaching philosophy statement and refer to it periodically to assess your progress and development as a Bible teacher.

Chapter Key Points

- Jesus' teaching was God-centered. He didn't teach to seek his own glory but the glory of the Father who sent him. He further explained, "Whoever speaks on their own does so to gain personal glory, but he who seeks the glory of the one who sent him is a man of truth; there is nothing false about him" (John 7:18 NIV).

- He was motivated by compassion for his students. That's the heart of student-centered teaching.

- The centrality of the Scriptures to our students' lives must be permanently fixed in our minds because understanding and applying the Scriptures will empower them to achieve Kingdom outcomes. It is good practice for the Bible teacher to consistently reflect on whether their teaching is empowering their students to know God, overcome the enemy, take dominion, and be transformed into the image of Christ.

- Every Bible teacher should articulate their teaching philosophy (the principles that guide their teaching ministry). Good practice dictates writing down the guiding principles that will direct you as you endeavor to fulfill your teaching ministry with excellence.

- A well-written teaching philosophy statement is a means of intently evaluating your teaching approach for continuous improvement. It empowers you to communicate your teaching beliefs and values to your students, peers, and leaders.

Reflect or Discuss

1. Who works harder in your classes, you or your students? If you want to incorporate student-centered teaching, should it be that way and why?

2. Do students in your classes have an opportunity to talk to the class about what they learn and defend their conclusions? What are some ways to accomplish this?

3. Do you ask your students questions, or do you only give them information? How can you incorporate questioning to get your students talking and involved?

4. Do any of the following quotes resonate with you and aspects of what you want your personal teaching

philosophy to be? Why? What other guiding principles do you think should be part of your teaching philosophy?

Education is the most powerful weapon which you can use to change the world. – Nelson Mandela

Education is not the filling of a pail, but the lighting of a fire. – William Butler Yeats

Who dares to teach must never cease to learn. – John Cotton Dana

Every teacher should have real world experience in the subject they teach. To teach science, you should now be or have been a scientist or been in a job that uses science a lot. To teach business, you should now be or have been an entrepreneur or worked in the corporate world. This way, we can teach for real life and not for tests or abstractions. — Hendrith Vanlon Smith, Jr.

Activity

Use the tips from this chapter to write a one-page personal teaching philosophy statement.

- It should describe what you believe about Bible teaching as it relates to your purpose and motives for being a Bible teacher.
- Articulate the objectives you are trying to achieve when teaching.

- Describe the methods you will use. Include concrete examples of what you will do in the classroom to support your purpose and beliefs. What methods will you employ?
- Describe the measures you will use to evaluate whether you remain true to your teaching purpose, values, and philosophy.

In the next chapter, you will apply everything you have learned to design a lesson plan for a Bible study or class that you and other Bible teachers can use.

Chapter 8

Designing Instruction: Lesson Plan Development

---

*The end of a matter is better than its beginning, and
patience is better than pride. (Ecclesiastes 7:8 NIV)*

The beginning of a lesson plan is in its expected end. One
of the reasons why God is a master planner is he knows
the end from the beginning. He used the mouth of his
prophet, Jeremiah, to say this, ". . . I know the thoughts that I
think toward you . . . thoughts of peace, and not of evil, to give
you an expected end" (Jeremiah 29:11 KJV). Part of your role as a
Bible teacher is to be a planner. You must plan your instruction
with the expected result you want for your students in mind.

The Five W's

So, to develop a lesson plan, start with the purpose—the why—
then move to the what, who, when, and where. Why and what are
you going to teach? You can, at first, state this in general terms.
However, you will later narrow it down and bring more definition
to your expected results in the form of learning objectives. Next,
consider who your audience will be and the where—the setting.
What tools, technology, and time will you have at your disposal?
When do you have to teach? How much time do you have to

prepare, and how much total time will you have to teach? Indicate this at the top of your lesson plan (see the sample lesson plan template in Appendix C).

The Learning Objectives

The expected results you want are called learning objectives. This is where your lesson plan begins—the things you expect students to learn or be able to do by the end of your teaching. Once you develop learning objectives, you can use them to select learning activities and evaluate whether students are progressing.

To write a learning objective, first, think about what you want students to learn or achieve by the end of your instruction time. For example, in general, you may want students to understand how to fast biblically. Once you have this broad goal, break it down into more detail by anticipating student questions and key information they will need to be successful. In this example, you might ask what is involved in knowing how to fast effectively.

Ask yourself what key information your students need to fast successfully and what questions they will likely have. Students will need to know what the Bible says about fasting and the heart attitudes and kind of fasting that pleases God. They will likely ask:

- How do you prepare for a fast? (Before)
- What should I do during a fast? (During)
- How do I properly break a fast? (After)
- Are there different lengths of fasting? (How long?)

As answers to these questions, you might form the following learning objectives for your Bible study. Please take note of the first word in each objective as it indicates the action you want the learner to be able to take:

1. Define biblical fasting.
   o If you want the student to be able to define biblical fasting, you must present or explain the definition in your content and check for their understanding.
2. Explain the different time lengths for fasting discussed in the Bible.
3. Identify the key attitudes needed for effective fasting in Scripture.
   o This objective means you want students to be able to locate/identify what the Bible says about the kind of heart attitude we should have when fasting. The first word of this objective is "identify," and that's important because it means "identify" is the action you want the learner to be able to take. Key Scripture passages for this objective might include Isaiah 58 and Jesus' teaching about fasting in Matthew 6.
4. Articulate how to prepare for a biblical fast.
   o This objective means you want students to be able to say, write, or articulate back to you how to prepare for a fast.
5. Discuss physical and spiritual hindrances to effective fasting.
   o Hopefully, it's becoming clear that this objective means that students need to discuss hindrances. That means you would need to prepare discussion questions, incorporate time for discussion in your lesson plan, or, if teaching online, create the discussion prompt in the online course space.
6. Analyze pitfalls to breaking a fast effectively.

Again, the verbs used at the beginning of each objective are important because they are actions students should be able to take during or after instruction, and your lesson plan needs to support those actions. In the world of education and instructional design, these verbs are part of a system of measurable verbs called Bloom's Taxonomy. If you want more information, you can see a list of Bloom's verbs in Appendix D. Also note, the idea is that the verbs are categorized into progressive levels of learning from basic comprehension to higher-level critical thinking and analysis.

Formulate Your Introduction or Hook and Content Presentation

Get students excited about what they are about to learn with an introduction or hook, and remember, you need to convince adults that what you are about to say is important and relevant. So make sure your introduction provides a rationale and explanation for the relevance of the topic and content. You can use a short quiz or poll to gauge prior knowledge, create a compelling question to confront misconceptions about the topic, or use a personal testimony or learning experience to introduce the topic and engage students.

Plan your main lecture or content presentation. Alternatives to traditional lectures include interviews, videos, and guest speakers.

Determine the Learning Activities

After you have formulated your learning objectives, use them to design the learning activities that will take place during instruction or afterwards as homework. For example, if one of your objectives is to define fasting, you know you will need to present content that includes the definition of fasting in the class introduction or lecture.

Likewise, if one of your objectives is for students to discuss physical and spiritual hindrances to effective fasting, you will need to include time in the lesson plan for students to share their experiences overcoming hindrances or discuss the challenges they have faced when fasting. Prepare a few discussion questions.

Plan Your Assessment or Check for Understanding

Before you conclude your class, be sure to check that students have learned key concepts and information. Think about the questions you can ask to ensure understanding or activities like small group presentations (one to three students briefly sharing) that can also communicate understanding.

Formulate Your Conclusion and Preview

Summarize the material and key points covered in class yourself or ask a student to do it. Explain anything they missed. Finally, preview the next class to foster excitement.

Assign a Realistic Timeframe for the Items in Your Lesson Plan

After you have planned the content, learning activities, knowledge check, conclusion, and preview, assign a realistic time limit to each element. This is why you need to know the total time you will have before you start your lesson plan.

By taking these steps, you will have all the information you need to complete your lesson plan:

1. Answer the Five W's.
2. Create the learning objectives.
3. Formulate your introduction or hook and content presentation.
4. Determine the learning activities.
5. Plan your assessment or knowledge check (check for understanding).
6. Formulate your conclusion and preview.
7. Assign a realistic timeframe for the items in your lesson plan.

You can use the following list of necessary items for a lesson plan to create your own template or use the sample lesson plan template in Appendix C.

Necessary Elements of a Lesson Plan

Audience Description

Date of Instruction / Length of Time for Instruction / Technology Tools

Objectives

Content (assign each item a time limit)

Introduction

Warm-up/Hook

Lecture or Other content presentation (interview, video)

Outline main points.

Examples/Illustrations/Stories

Activities

Check for Understanding /Assessment /
Knowledge Check /

Conclusion and Preview

Note: This chapter includes an activity to use the information in
the chapter to create a lesson plan for a Bible class you and other
Bible teachers can use. Please do not skip it. Instead, create your
lesson plan and share it with another Bible teacher for feedback
and discussion.

Before you create the lesson plan, take a moment to review this
chapter's key points. Then, reflect individually or discuss the
questions with other Bible teachers.

Chapter Key Points

- Part of your role as a Bible teacher is to be a planner. You
  must plan your instruction with the expected result you
  want for your students in mind.
- The expected results you want are called learning
  objectives. This is where your lesson plan begins—the
  things you expect students to learn or be able to do by the
  end of your teaching.
- Use verbs from Bloom's Taxonomy as the first word of a
  learning objective (See Appendix D).
- Use the following steps to create a lesson plan:
  1. Answer the Five W's.
  2. Create the learning objectives.
  3. Formulate your introduction or hook and content
     presentation.
  4. Determine the learning activities.

5. Plan your assessment or knowledge check (check for understanding).
6. Formulate your conclusion and preview.
7. Assign a realistic timeframe for the items in your lesson plan.

Reflect or Discuss

1. Planning and preparation are required for excellence in Bible teaching. What kind of discipline is needed for effective lesson planning and study? What schedule changes, if any, will you need to make to consistently incorporate lesson planning into your teaching ministry?

Activity

Use the information from this chapter to create a lesson plan for a Bible class. Then, share it with another Bible teacher for feedback and discussion.

In the next and final chapter, we discuss what it means to be called into the teaching ministry. We must each accept the invitation to the calling.

Chapter 9

A Grace, a Call, an Invitation, and a Charge

As each one has received a gift, minister it to one another, as good stewards of the manifold grace of God. [11] If anyone speaks, let him speak *as the oracles of God. If anyone ministers,* let him do it *as with the ability which God supplies, that in all things God may be glorified through Jesus Christ, to whom belong the glory and the dominion forever and ever. Amen. (1 Peter 4:10-11 NKJV)*

You have made it the final chapter. Congratulations! The pages you have read thus far as well as the reflections and activities were written to train believers with a teaching grace to serve their gift in excellence. In Chapter 1, we said:

This book was . . . written to you as if you have been called to the teaching ministry, and you must realize how vital your ministry is to the expansion of the kingdom. What if the next great Kathryn Kuhlman, Billy Graham, neighborhood evangelist, or Sunday School teacher is sitting in one of your classes? What impact will you make on their lives? Every time you teach, you have an opportunity to impact the kingdom—please do not overlook your potential or take it for granted. Sit up; rise up, shake yourself, and welcome yourself once again to the teaching ministry.

As we conclude, I again welcome you to the teaching ministry. But this time, I welcome you to walk in the grace that has been bestowed upon you. The teaching ministry is a ministry of grace. In 1 Peter 4:10, the apostle admonishes us to be good stewards of the manifold grace of God by serving our gifts (our grace) to one another.

A Grace

If you are graced to teach, God has broken off a piece of his multifaceted grace and placed it down inside you. The grace gift of teaching is a grace magnet. When you are graced to teach, you become a magnet. People are drawn to you and ask you questions about the Bible seemingly for no reason. You are graced to impart knowledge in understandable language. People testify that you helped them understand the Scriptures better.

Likely, you are graced to research and study the Bible for hours at a time. You can easily lose yourself and track of time in study. Books seem to be your best friends. You hate to let people borrow them, and when you do, you are emphatic that they return them. If this description fits you, you are likely graced to teach.

Jesus, full of grace, was the Master Teacher. The teaching grace was inside of him, who was the fullness of the godhead bodily. That means a piece of God's grace has been given to you to do what Jesus did—you have received grace to teach, and you must steward it well.

Don't waste the grace! Be disciplined. Apply yourself to develop, hone, strengthen, and sharpen your grace. Stir up the gift of God inside of you. You are gifted. You are graced. Embrace it. Own it. Hone it. Serve it.

- Embrace it: Determine to understand, discover, and activate (stir up) your giftedness by faith.
- Own it: Drive out any doubt about your giftedness, and answer the call.
- Hone it: Develop your gift(s). Add skill to the raw grace. Learn the craft, protocols, and nuances of teaching.
- Serve it: Serve your teaching gift to the Church and humanity.

A Call and an Invitation

Your entry into the teaching ministry begins with embracing it and owning it. To own it, you must answer the call. Many people say, "I'm called," but don't realize a calling is an invitation. You must answer the invitation before you can begin. You must RSVP; and the only way you can RSVP is to own the call to the teaching ministry as your own personal invitation that you honor—RSVP to—daily. This is why answering the call requires consistence and diligence: Consider the diligence mentioned in the following passage of Scripture.

> But also for this very reason, *giving all diligence*, add to your faith virtue, to virtue knowledge, [6] to knowledge self-control, to self-control perseverance, to perseverance godliness, [7] to godliness brotherly kindness, and to brotherly kindness love. [8] For if these things are yours and abound, *you* will be neither barren nor unfruitful in the knowledge of our Lord Jesus Christ. [9] For he who lacks

these things is shortsighted, even to blindness, and has forgotten that he was cleansed from his old sins. [10] Therefore, brethren, *be even more diligent to make your call and election sure*, for if you do these things you will never stumble; [11] for so an entrance will be supplied to you abundantly into the everlasting kingdom of our Lord and Savior Jesus Christ. (2 Peter 1:5-11 NKJV, italics added)

Will you be diligent?

Bible teacher, give all diligence to your teaching ministry. Be even more diligent to make your call and election sure, so an entrance will be supplied to you abundantly into the everlasting Kingdom of our Lord and Savior Jesus Christ.

A Charge

I charge you to prioritize your entrance into the Kingdom, and the Kingdom itself. Embrace and impart a Kingdom Worldview. Remember your Kingdom responsibilities as a Bible teacher:

- *Responsibility One: Be a doer of what you teach.* (James 2:26-3:1)
- *Responsibility Two: Come up higher, repent quicker, and change faster than others. Cultivate repentance as a lifestyle.* (Luke 12:47-48)
- *Responsibility Three: Let the Word of God transform you first. Focus on continual transformation to avoid self-deception.* (Romans 12:2)
- *Responsibility Four: Be mature in your words. Discipline your tongue, mature in your word choices, and develop your vocabulary.* (John 6:63, Matthew 12:34)
- *Responsibility Five: Before you present your teaching to men, present yourself to God. Focus on pleasing him, not impressing men.* (2 Timothy 2:15)

- *Responsibility Six: Use the proper tools to rightly divide the Word of Truth.* (2 Timothy 2:15)
- *Responsibility Seven: Seek to excel at teaching (not merely getting by) by continuous equipping.* (2 Timothy 3:16-17)

Remember that Jesus, our Master Teacher, was a God-and-student-centered teacher moved by compassion for his students. Make kingdom compassion your central motivation.

Finally, you can do all things through Christ, your Master Teacher. He is making intercession for you. The great cloud of witnesses is cheering for you, and so am I. Go and teach all nations, play your teaching part in the Great Commission, and may God himself eternally reward you, in Jesus' name.

If this book has been a blessing to you, send your testimony to pastorlenita@gmail.com. God abundantly bless you!

Appendix A: Sample Christian Education Program Design

A Christian Education program should be formulated from learning objectives. For example, based on the four critical truths of the Kingdom Worldview in Chapter Four, Christian Education must focus on preparing a people to:

- Know their Creator!
- Overcome the enemy's wiles, so they don't fall like Adam and Eve.
- Redeem the earth by exercising their dominion mandate.
- Be transformed and conformed to the image of Christ.

A program comprised of a series of adult Sunday School classes can be developed from these four objectives. For example, a church could develop a program containing the following courses and help their adult members progress through them, awarding a certificate for each. They could also require a member to complete all these classes before they could serve in leadership:

0 • Membership Class: Embracing the Vision

1 • Foundations of the Faith: Understanding God's Heart for Salvation

2 • Intimacy with God: Faith, Fellowship, and Devotion

3 • Victory Over the Enemy: Understanding the Believer's Authority and Weapons

4 • The Dominion Mandate: God's Original Purpose for Mankind and Earth

5 • Servant Leadership: Conformed to His Image

Please note that these classes map back to the four focuses of the Kingdom Worldview.

Class Zero: Membership Class: Embracing the Vision

This class addresses membership and assimilation objectives, helping the new member understand the church vision and mission, membership expectations, how the church worships, church doctrines such as communion, giving, water baptism, and their Romans 12 spiritual gifts.

Class One: Foundations of the Faith: Understanding God's Heart for Salvation

This class focuses on the assurance of salvation and sharing our faith. Christian education should emphasize sharing our faith early and often to reveal the Heavenly Father's heart. Topics could include Christ's compassion, friendship evangelism, co-worker evangelism, and participating in Matthew 25 activities such as feeding the hungry (church food bank), clothing the naked, praying for the sick, and prison ministry.

Class Two: Intimacy with God: Faith, Fellowship, and Devotion

This class's focus is intimately knowing God as Heavenly Father. Topics include coming to God with faith, believing he is who he says he is, the Cross as a means of restored fellowship with God, and how to cultivate a life of devotion through quiet times, personal devotions, a consistent prayer life, and knowing how and what to pray.

Class Three: Victory Over the Enemy: Understanding the Believer's Authority and Weapons

This class focuses on helping the believer overcome the enemy's wiles. A key passage of Scripture is Ephesians 6:10-19. Help the believer understand their armor and weapons, how to resist the enemy, and how to win the battle of the mind and against the flesh.

Class Four: The Dominion Mandate: God's Original Purpose for Mankind and Earth

Explore the four imperatives of the Genesis 1:26-28 dominion mandate and help the believer understand that, despite Adam's fall, Jesus has brought restoration and empowered us to walk in this mandate today.

Class Five: Servant Leadership: Conformed to His Image

The passage in John 13 is crucial for every believer to understand Jesus' servanthood heart and emulate it. Every believer must have a servant's spirit and conform to the image of Christ, who humbled himself and served humanity.

Additional subsequent classes might include:

- The Dominion Mandate: Biblical Financial Stewardship
- How to Lead a Cell Group

Appendix B: Sample Student Questionnaire
(Pre-class or First class)

Sample Student Survey

1. Do you have a Bible that is easy to read and understand?
   Yes____ No____

2. Do you have transportation to class?
   Yes____ No____

3. What is the last level of education you completed?
   Elementary____ Middle School_____ High School____
   College____ Graduate School____

4. How comfortable are you with using email, Zoom, and MS Word? Please indicate if you need assistance.
   Comfortable____ Very Comfortable____ I need assistance____

5. How comfortable are you with using computers in general?
   Comfortable____ Very Comfortable____ I need assistance____

6. What's the best way to contact you?
   Cell Phone Call____ Email____ Text____

7. Which class activities do you most enjoy?
   General Discussion____ Group Discussion____ Individual
   Presentation____ Group Presentation____
   Videos____ Guest Speakers____

8. Is there anything else you'd like me to know to better help you learn?

Appendix C: Sample Lesson Plan Template

Overall Subject/Purpose:	
Date Instruction to be Delivered:	Total Time for Instruction:
Class Location: Classroom Seating Setup:	Technology Tools Available:
Audience Description:	

Learning Objectives:
Starter or Introduction: Pre-assessments, questionnaires?
Warm-up/Hook:
Lecture or Other content presentation (interview, video, guest speaker) Outline main points. Examples/Illustrations/Stories.

Main Activity 1	Main Activity 2
Group Work or Discussion Questions:	

Check for Understanding / Assessment / Knowledge Check:
Conclusion and Preview:
Homework:

Appendix D: Bloom's Taxonomy

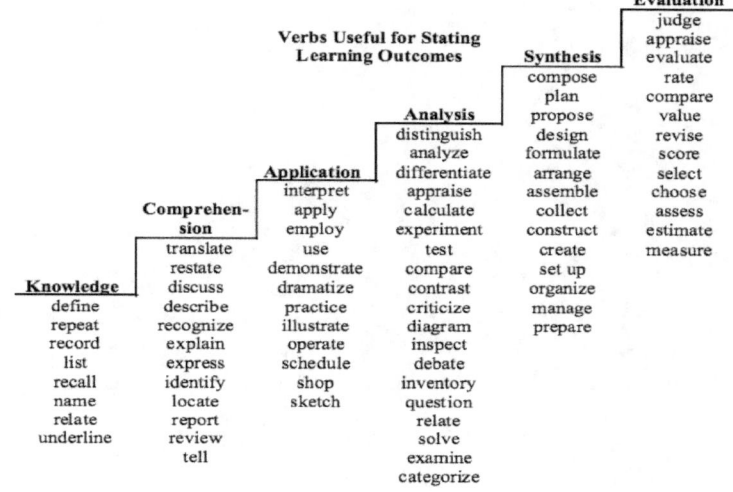

Source: Bloom, B. (1973). Taxonomy of Educational Objectives

Appendix E: Additional Resources

Berkhof Louis, *Foundations of Christian education: Addresses to Christian teachers* (Phillipsburg, N.J: Presbyterian and Reformed Pub. Co., 1989)

Chris Hermans, Isolde Driesen, and Aad de Jong, "Towards a Typology of General Aims of Christian Adult Education," *Journal of Empirical Theology* 18, no. 2 (2005): XXXX, https://doi.org/10.1163/157092505774649243.

Kathryn Yvonne Price, "Preparing new members for a life of Christian discipleship in a moderate-sized African American Holiness-Pentecostal church" (DigitalCommons@Robert W. Woodruff Library, Atlanta University Center, 2000), XXXX, http://digitalcommons.auctr.edu/dissertations/A AIDP14684.

Michael J. Anthony, *Exploring the history and philosophy of Christian education: Principles for the 21st century* (Grand Rapids, MI: Kregel Publications, 2003)

About the Author

Lenita Reeves has over twenty years of Christian teaching experience as an adult Sunday School teacher, cell group leader, women's ministry leader, associate pastor, intercessory and prophetic trainer, and lead pastor. She also has over ten years of professional, corporate instructional design experience and has served as an adjunct faculty member and teacher trainer.

She is the senior pastor of Action Chapel North Carolina, and Action Chapel Baltimore, prophetic churches under the covering of Archbishop Nicholas Duncan-Williams, who ordained her into ministry.

She is the author of several books including, *I Am: The Divine Purpose Manifesto, Fervent Fire, Breaking the Silence, The Spirit of Rejection, and I Am a Creative, Speaking Spirit.* And she is the founder of PurposeHouse Publishing, which helps others publish their books and meet their marketing needs.

As an abuse survivor and former teen mom, God has graced Lenita to be an outspoken overcomer, sharing her testimony freely and as a result, seeing captives set free all over the world. She is an international conference speaker and a member of the RAINN speaker's bureau. She has travelled the world to conduct apostolic missions and train leaders in London, Jamaica, Haiti, the Bahamas, Kenya, Uganda, and Ghana.

She began her service to the Lord in campus ministry. As Deputy Director of Campus Ministries United, she assisted in planting campus branches and the coordination of an annual conference aimed at bringing various campus ministries together in a night of prayer, praise, and relationship building. In the next phase of her ministry, God taught her the basics of pastoring while serving as a youth minister.

Some call her preacher, and some call her teacher, but all agree that she is a prolific, prophetic, and apostolic voice who speaks with transparency, highlighting her highs as well as her lows to show others that God can turn pain into a platform and use the foolish things of this world to confound the wise.

From senior class president to director in Corporate America to founder of a non-profit and pastor, leadership has been an evident mark of Pastor Lenita's life calling and passions. She has a Bachelor of Science in Industrial Engineering from Georgia Tech, a Master of Arts in Dance Education from the Ohio State University and an MBA from the University of Maryland, College Park. She is currently a doctoral candidate in Christian Counselling and attended Beulah Heights Bible College in Atlanta, Georgia, which was then under the leadership of Dr. Sam Chand.

She is married to Cephas Reeves, and they have four children, Elijah, Cenita, Ethan, and Joshua.

For more information, visit www.lenitareeves.org.

Other Titles

- *Fervent Fire: Understanding the Pattern of the Priesthood for Prevailing Intercessory Prayer*
- *The Spirit of Rejection: Heal its wounds, Restore your Self-Esteem, and Move on to Promotion*
- *Breaking the Silence: The Journey from Rape to Redemption*
- *An Anchor for My Soul: Soul-stabilizing Devotions for the Multi-tasked Woman*
- *Understanding the Power of Agreement: A Necessary Key for Prayer, Relationships, and Progress*

Online Courses

- *School of Intercession 101: The Priesthood of Intercession*
- *School of Intercession 102: Activating Spiritual Gifts for Targeted Intercession*
- *Now Discover Purpose: 80 Days to Stop Wondering, Unleash Yor Purpose Design and Create a 365-Day Plan to Live on Purpose*

Stay Connected

Discover the latest tools and encouragement for living on purpose! Visit www.lenitareeves.org and join our mailing list for the latest blog posts and continued news and previews of other upcoming books.

Visit us on Social Media

Facebook/ Instagram/ YouTube: @pastorlenita

www.ingramcontent.com/pod-product-compliance
Lightning Source LLC
Chambersburg PA
CBHW071021120626
46546CB00003B/1186